I See LOVE

© 2022 Jenny Phillips
goodandbeautiful.com
Cover design by Kayla Ellingsworth

Written by
David Wiseman

Illustrated by
Alessia Turchie

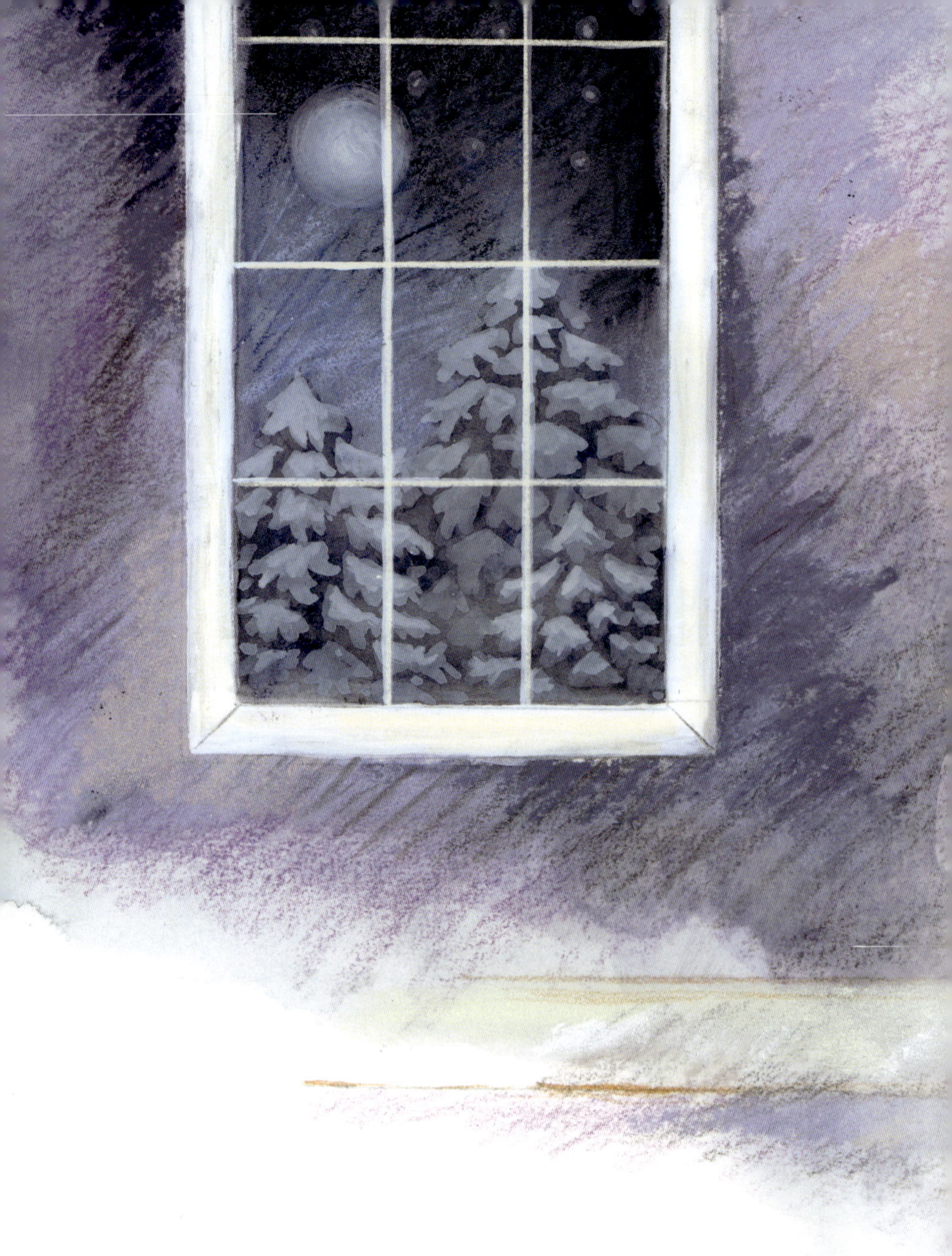

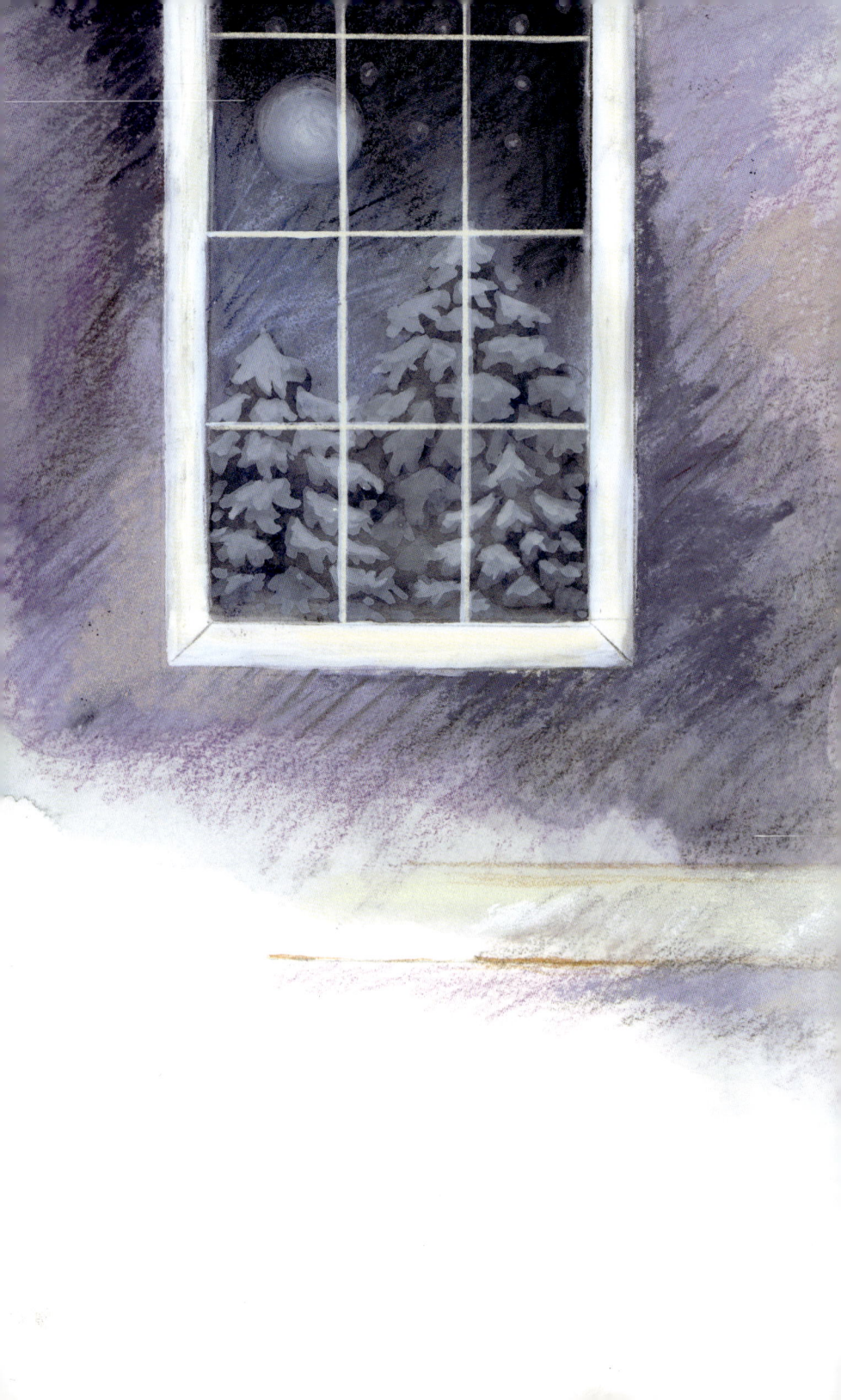

Challenge Words:

beauty

blanket

everywhere

mountain

Each day, as I look up and down,

I see beauty all around.

I see grass and kids at play.

I see the clouds slip away.

The more I look, the more can be found.

I see beauty all around.

I look up, and I see the sky.

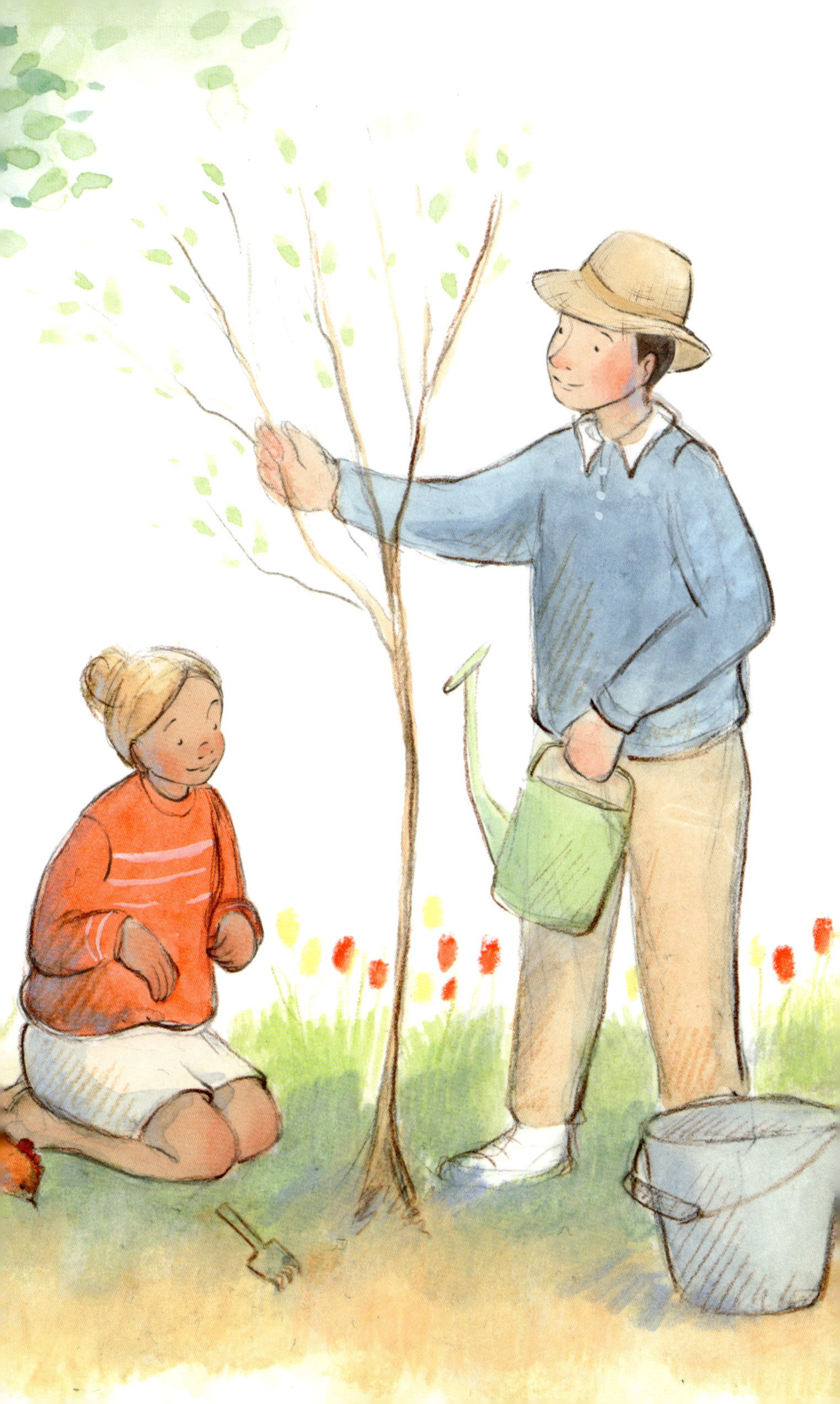

I look down at a dog passing by.

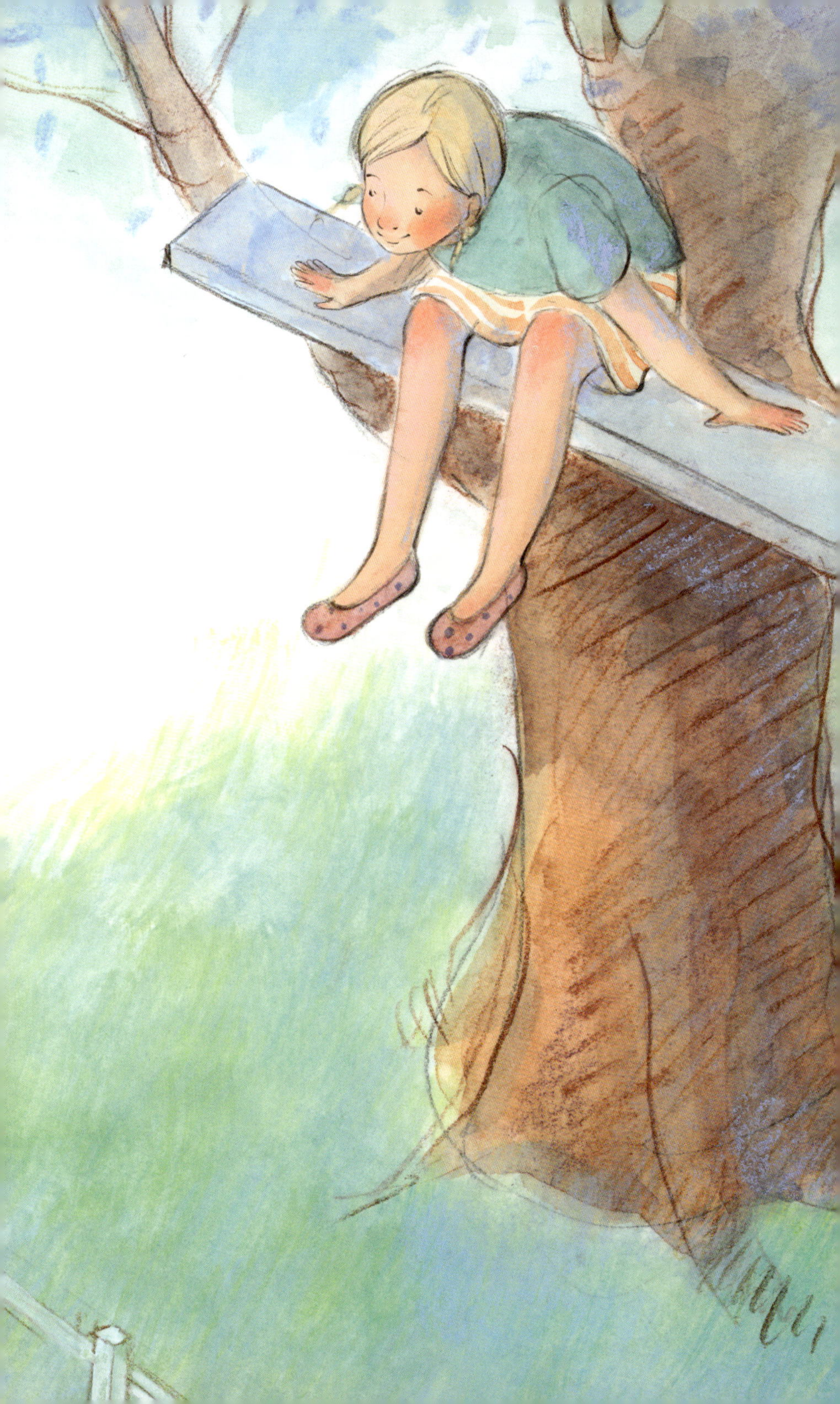

I look up and see birds fly free.

I look down at a buzzing bee.

Each day, as I look up and down,

I see beauty all around.

I see girls singing songs aloud.

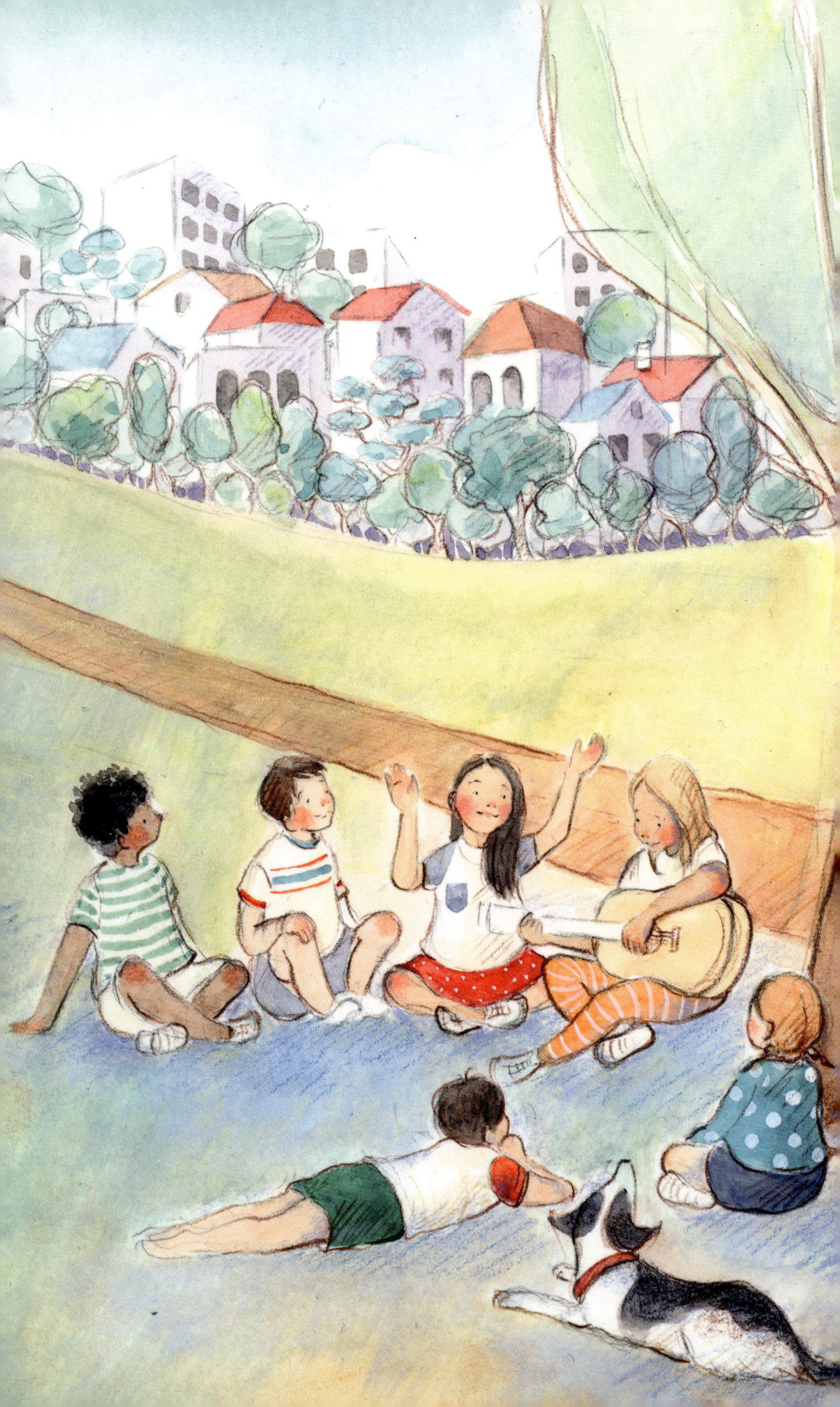

I see boys throwing balls on the ground.

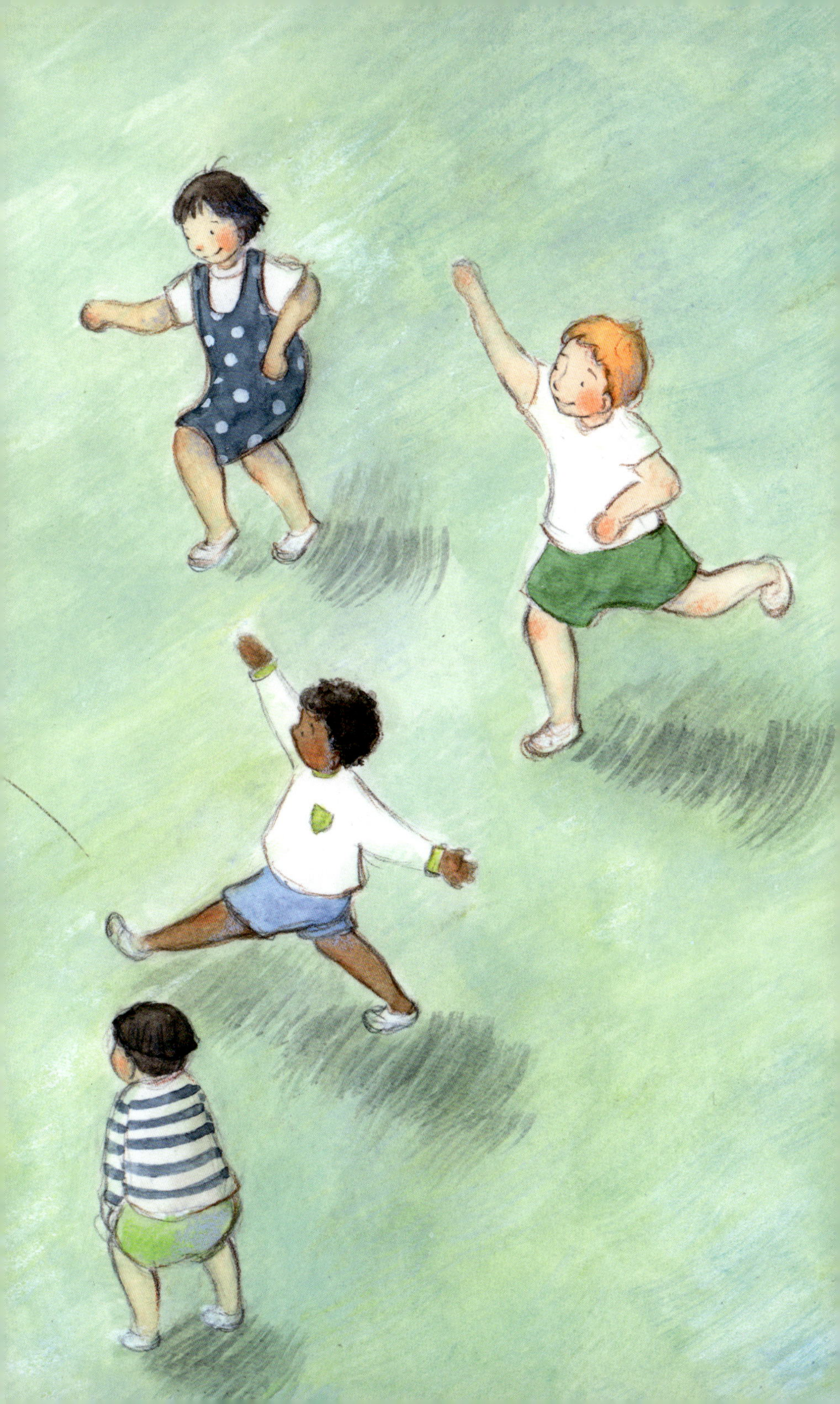

I see beauty all around.

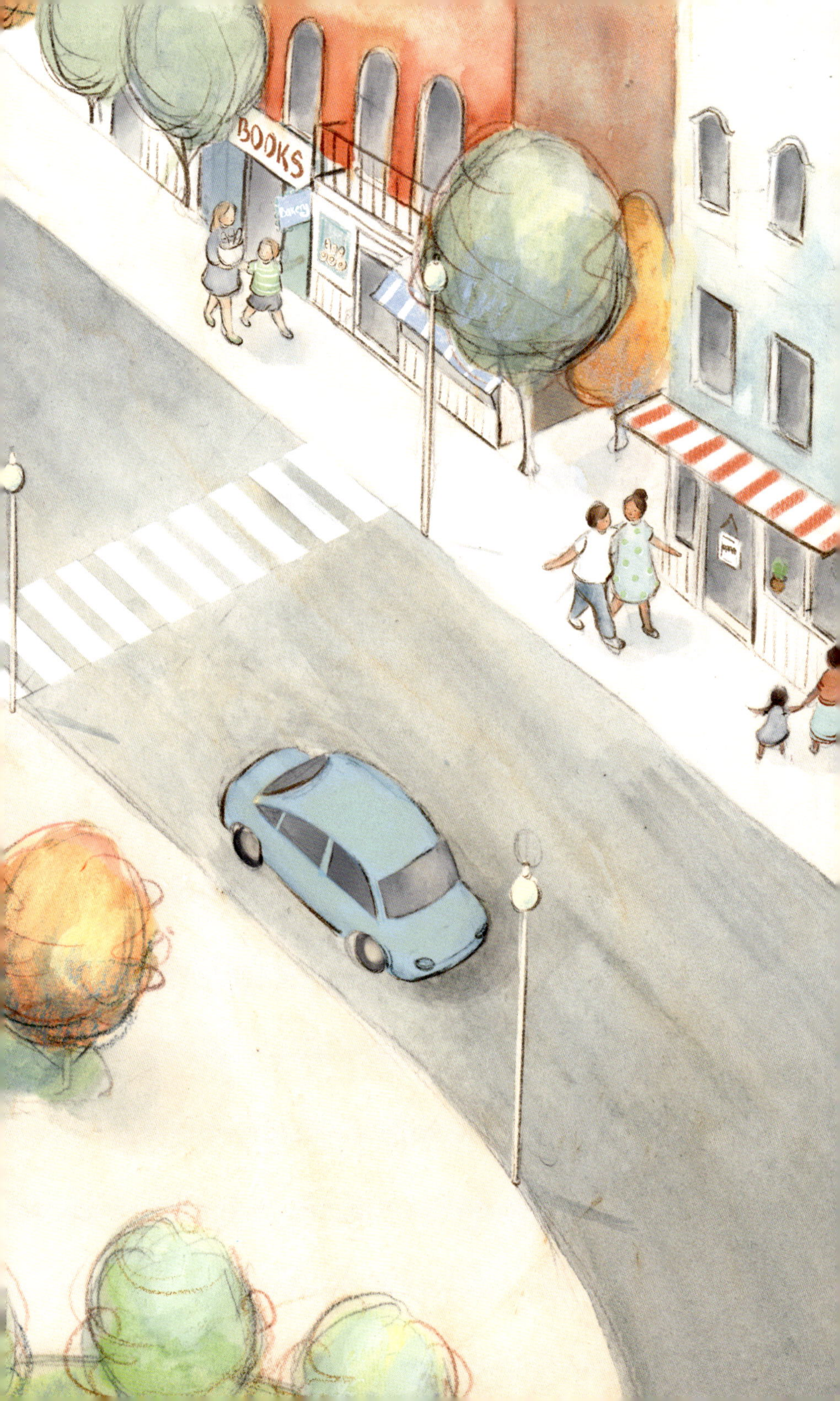

I look up, and I see the leaves.

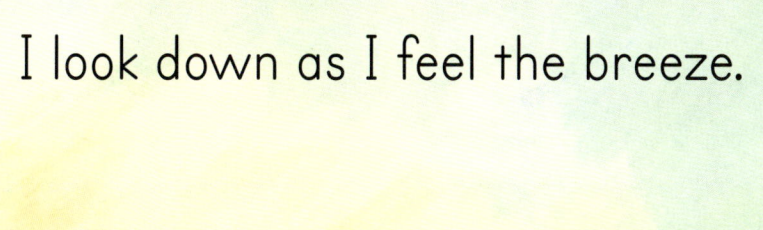

I look down as I feel the breeze.

I look up, and I see a star.

I look down at the hills so far.

Each day, as I look up and down,

I see beauty all around.

I see a park at the end
of the way.

I see a baby, and she likes to play.

Each time I look,

joy is found.

I see beauty all around.

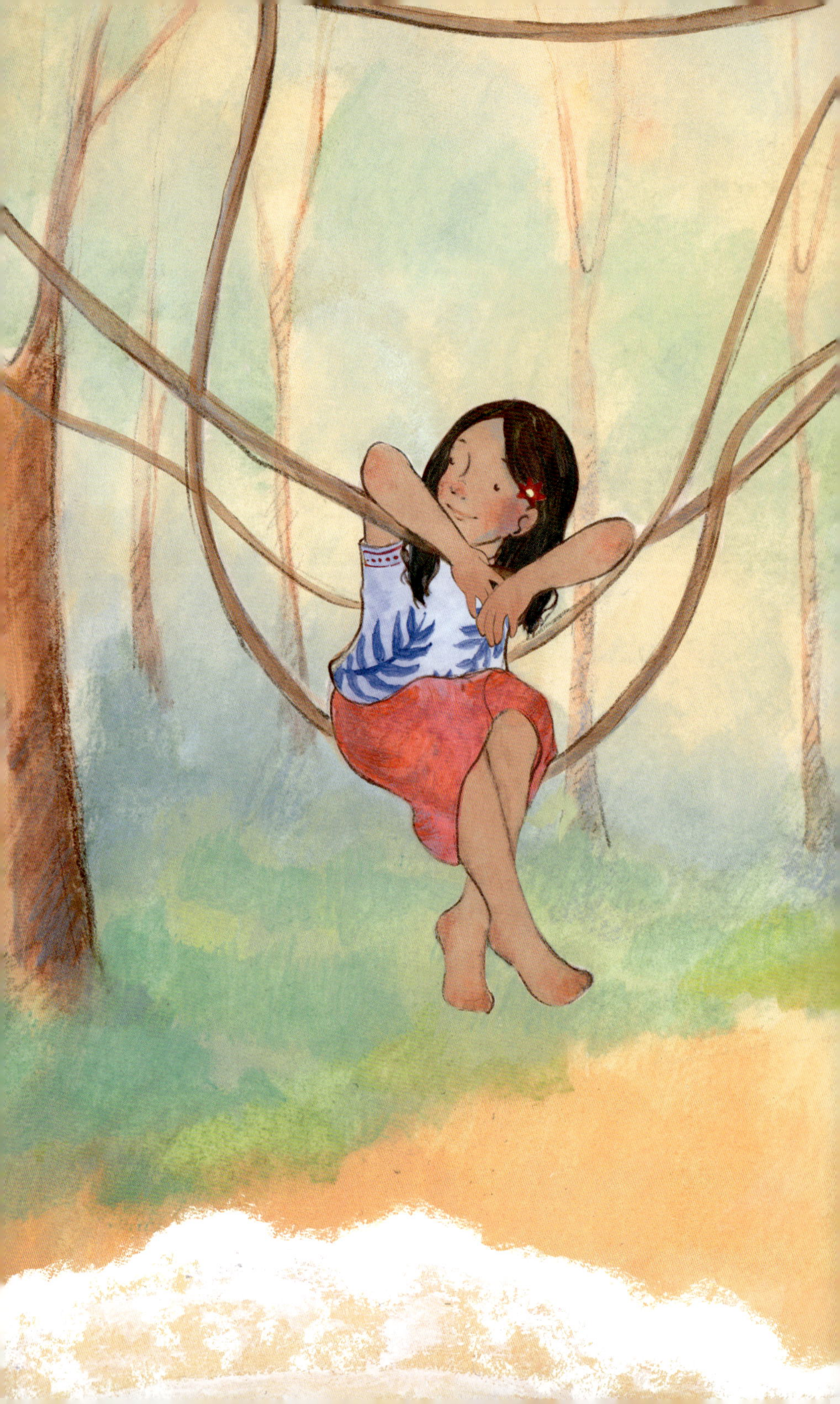

I look up as the sun starts the day.

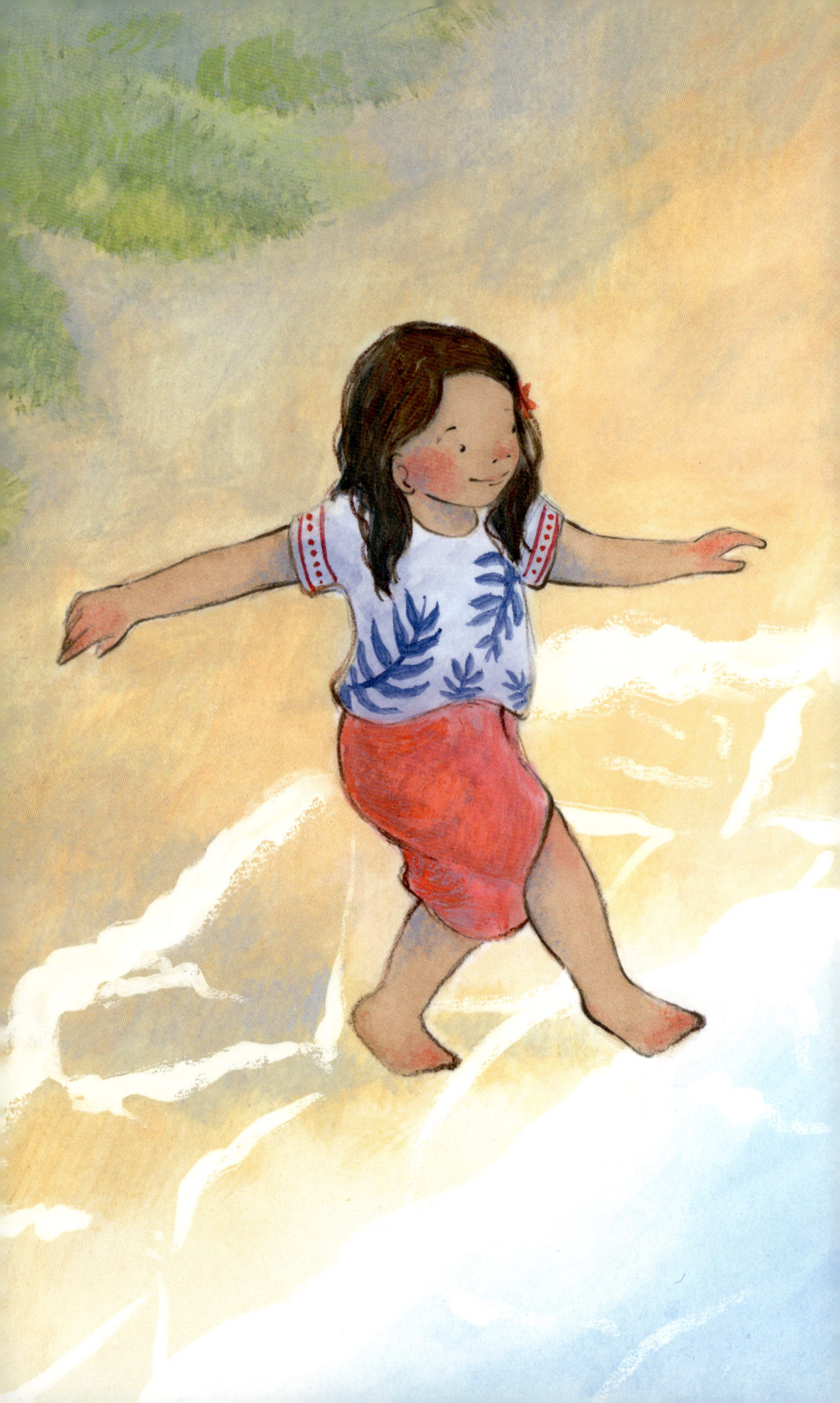

I look down at the sea spray.

I look up to the mountain peak.

I look down at

ants that sneak.

Each day, as I look up and down,

I see beauty all around.

I see a fire,
warm and red.

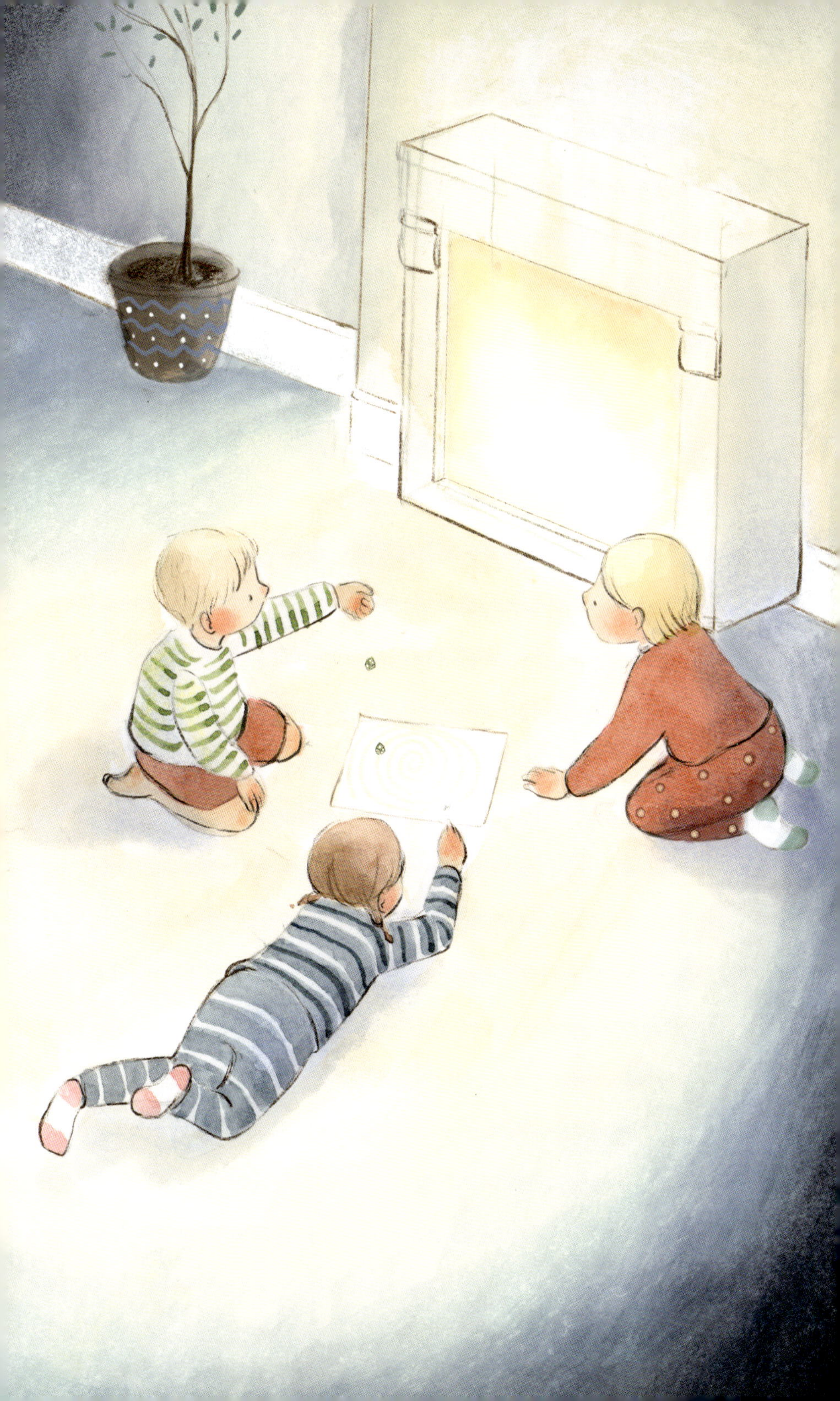

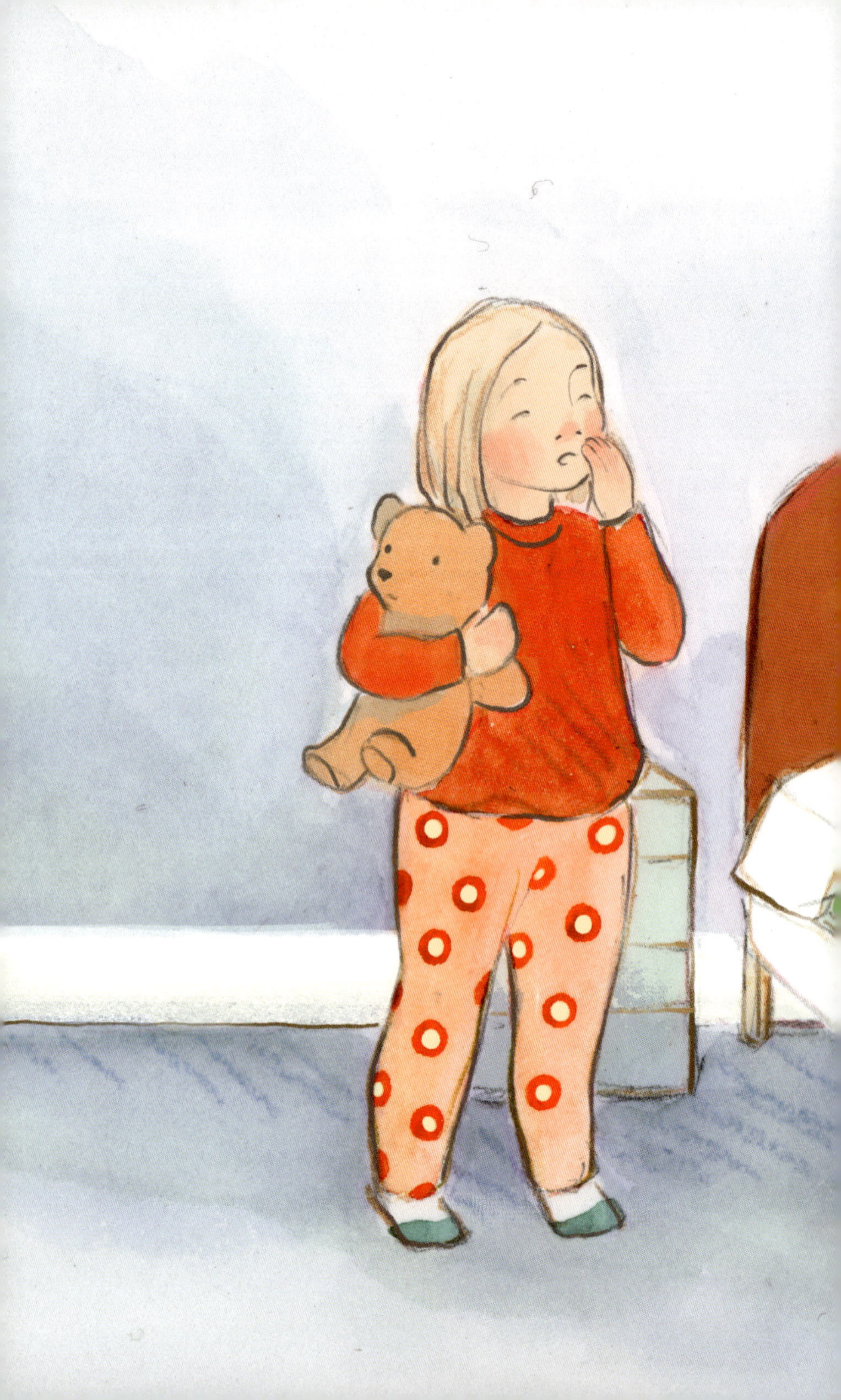

I see a blanket on my bed.

I see rest after work and play.

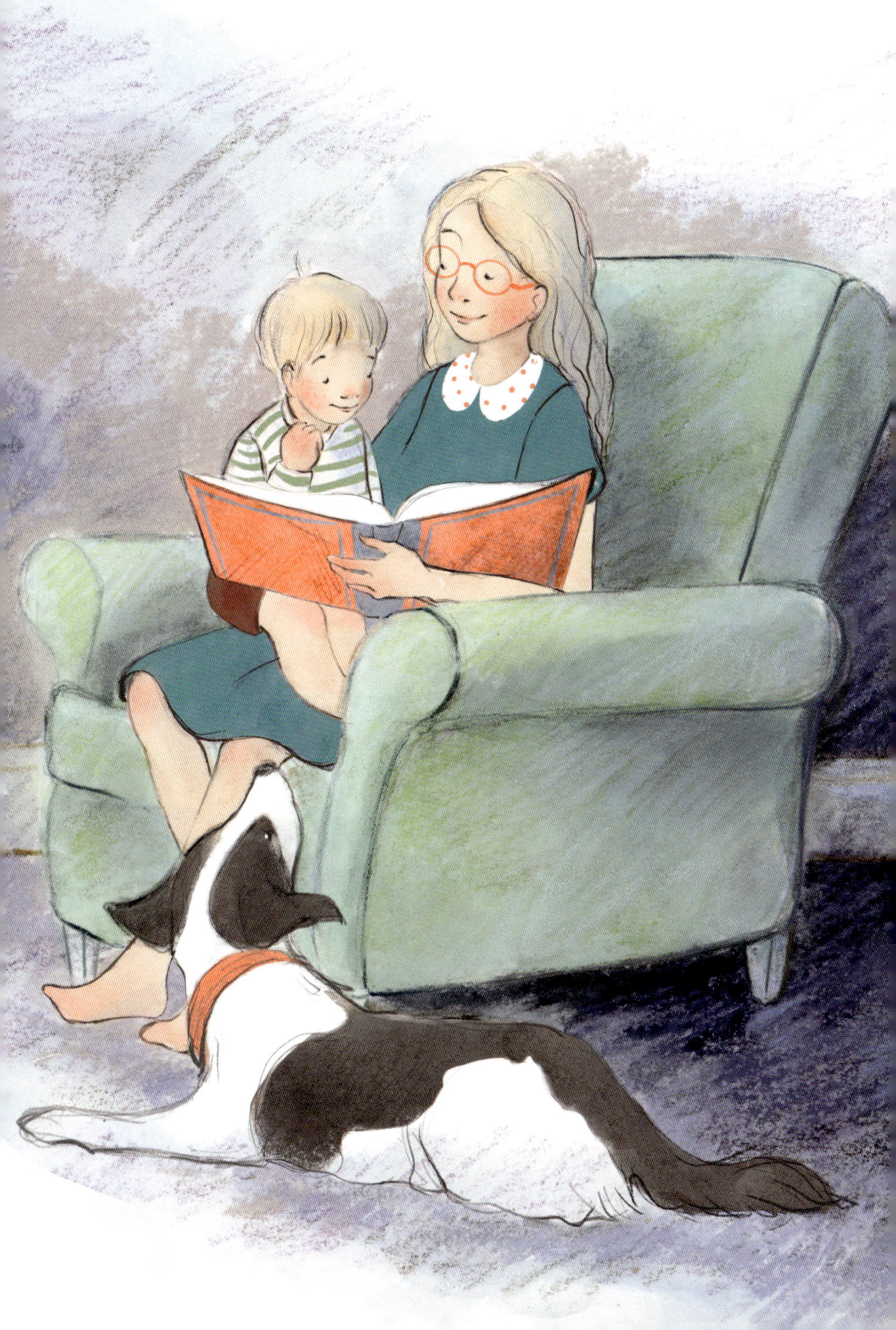

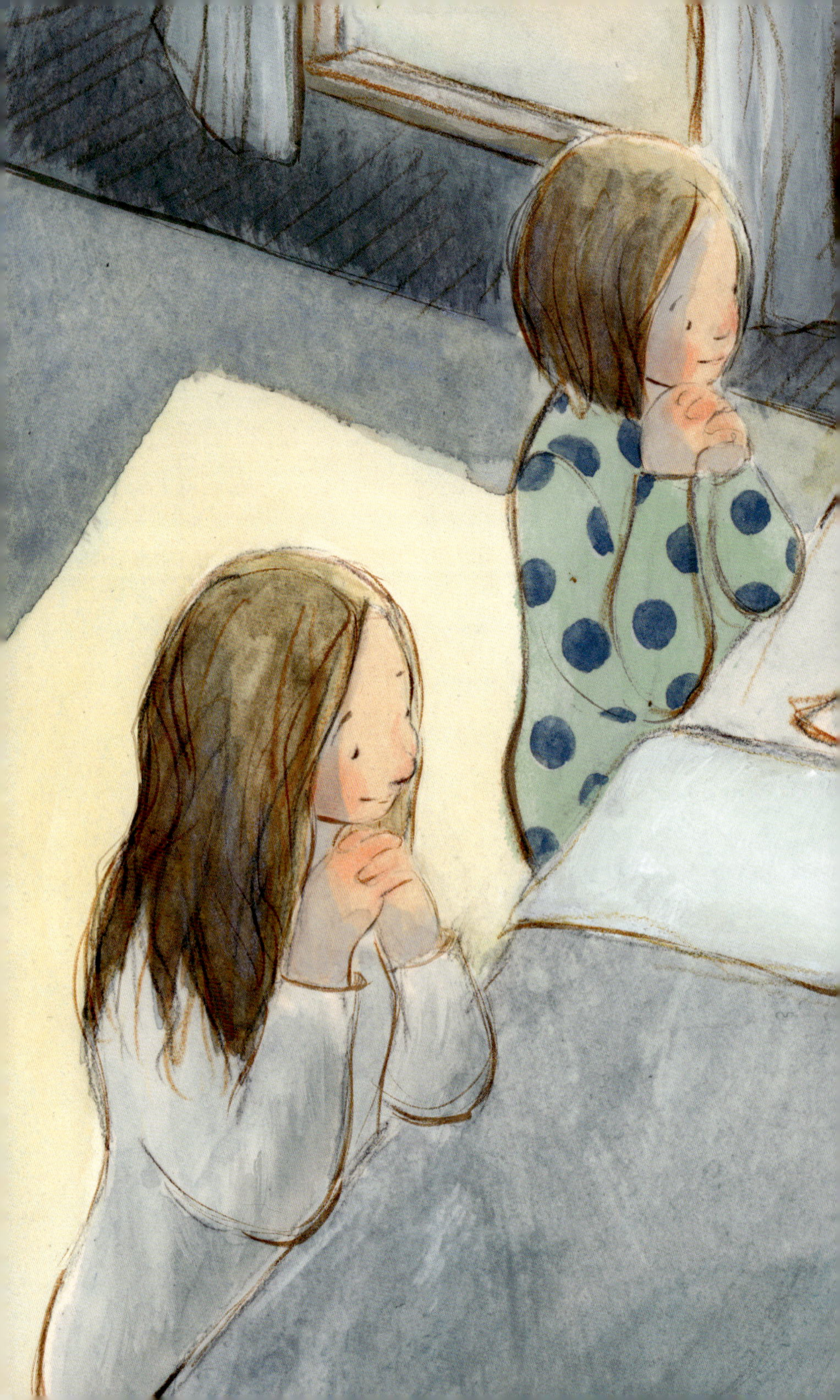

I see prayer at the end of the day.

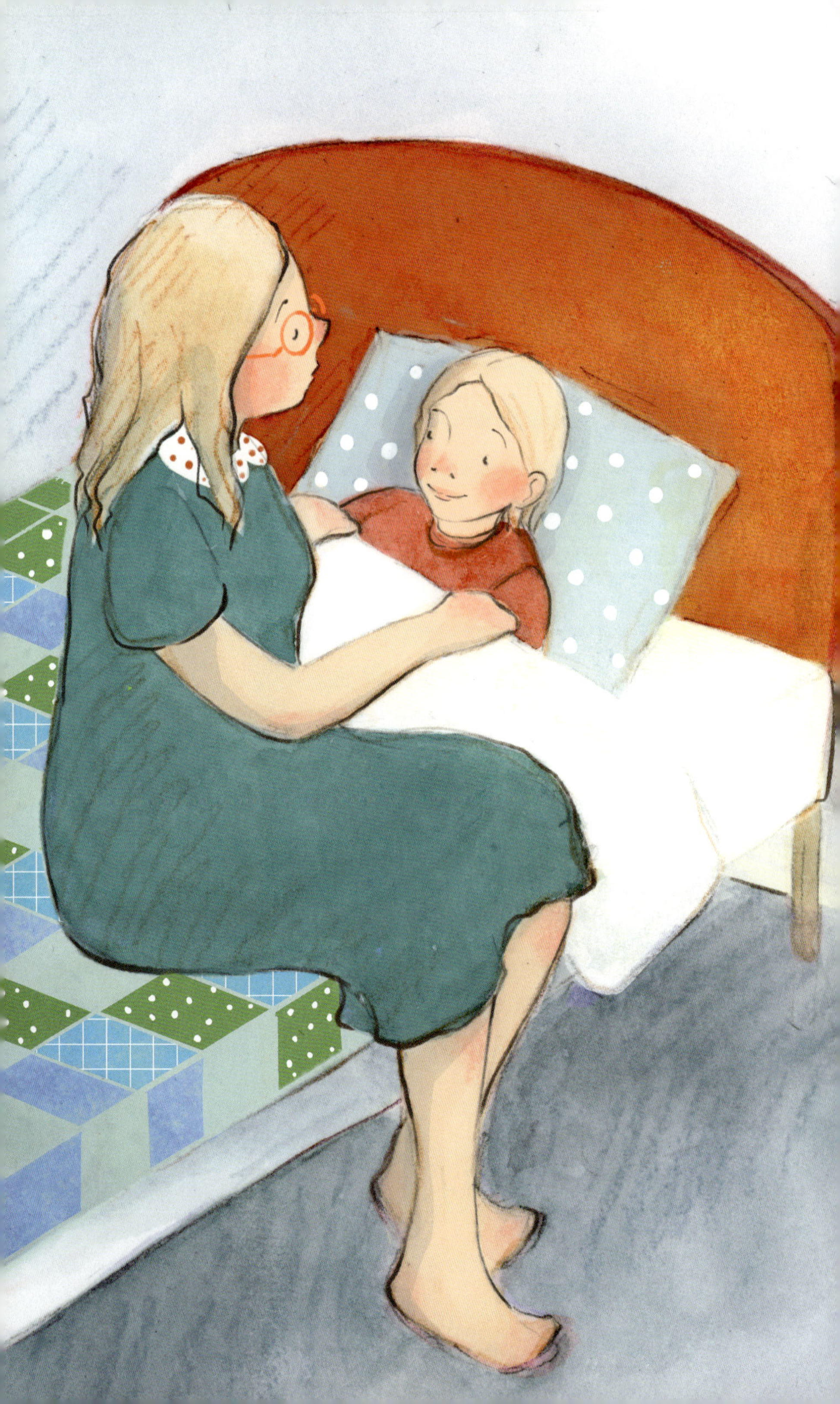

At home, I look, and love is found.

I see beauty all around.

I close my eyes, and love is there.

I see beauty everywhere.

It is on the ground.

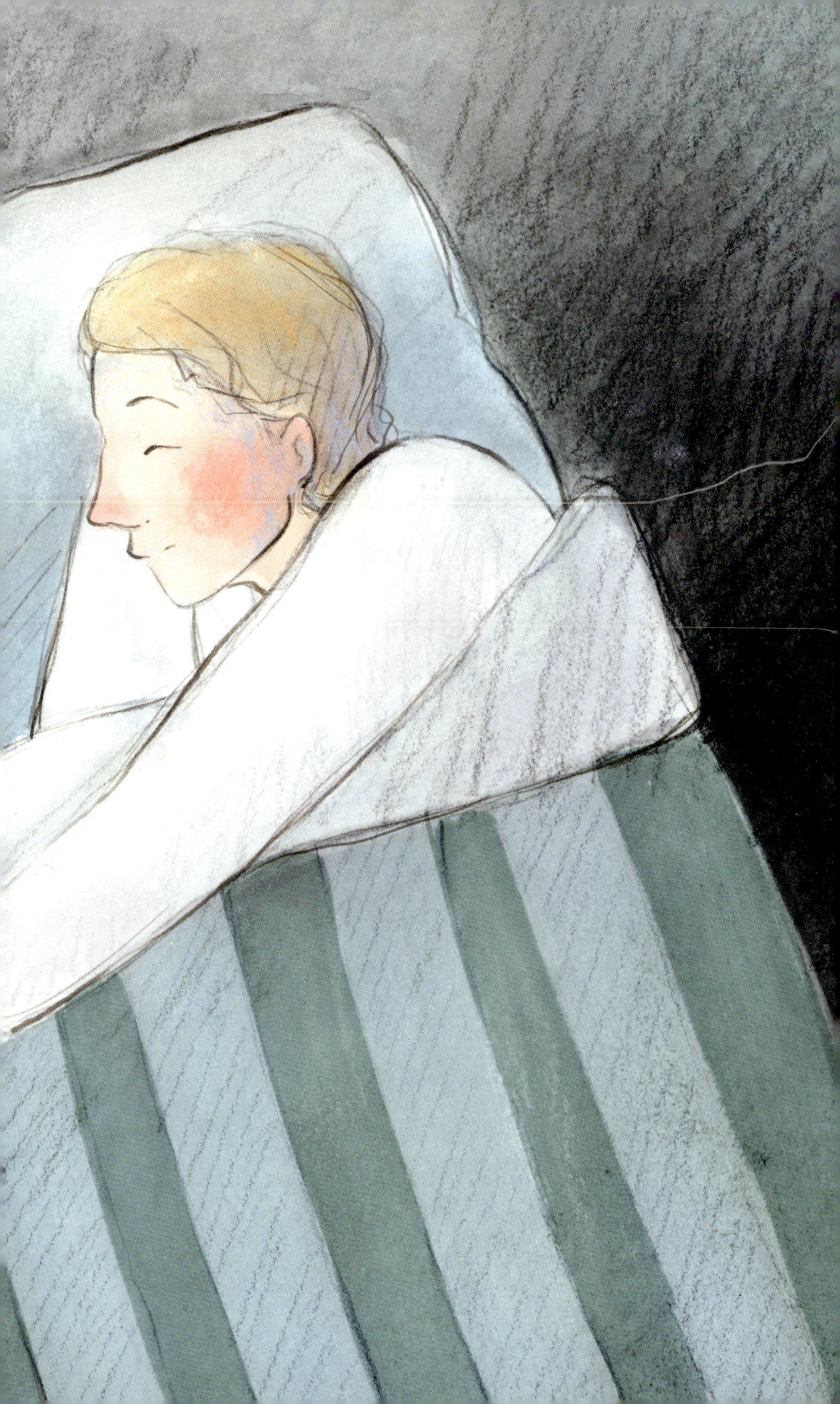

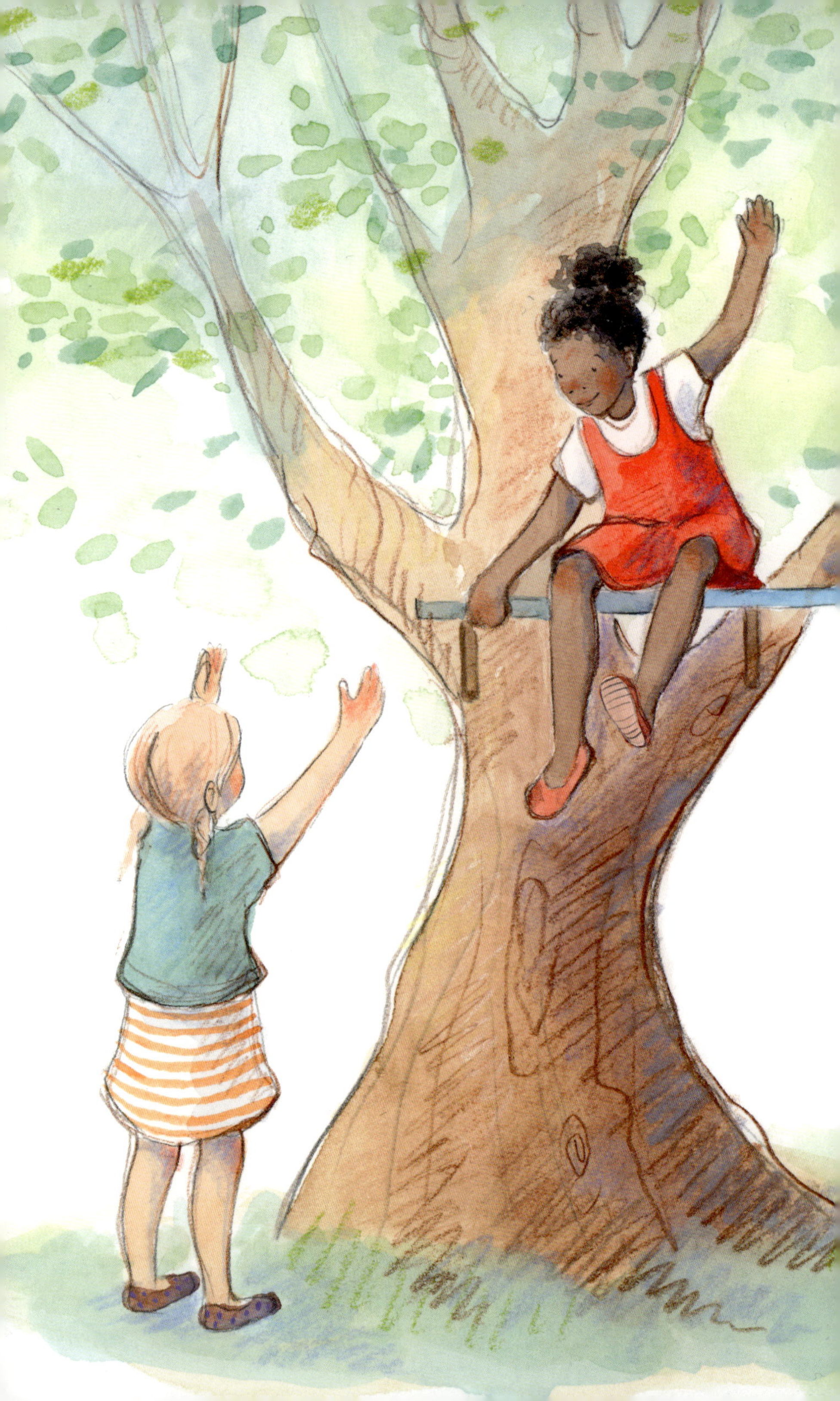

It is up above.

In it all, I see love.

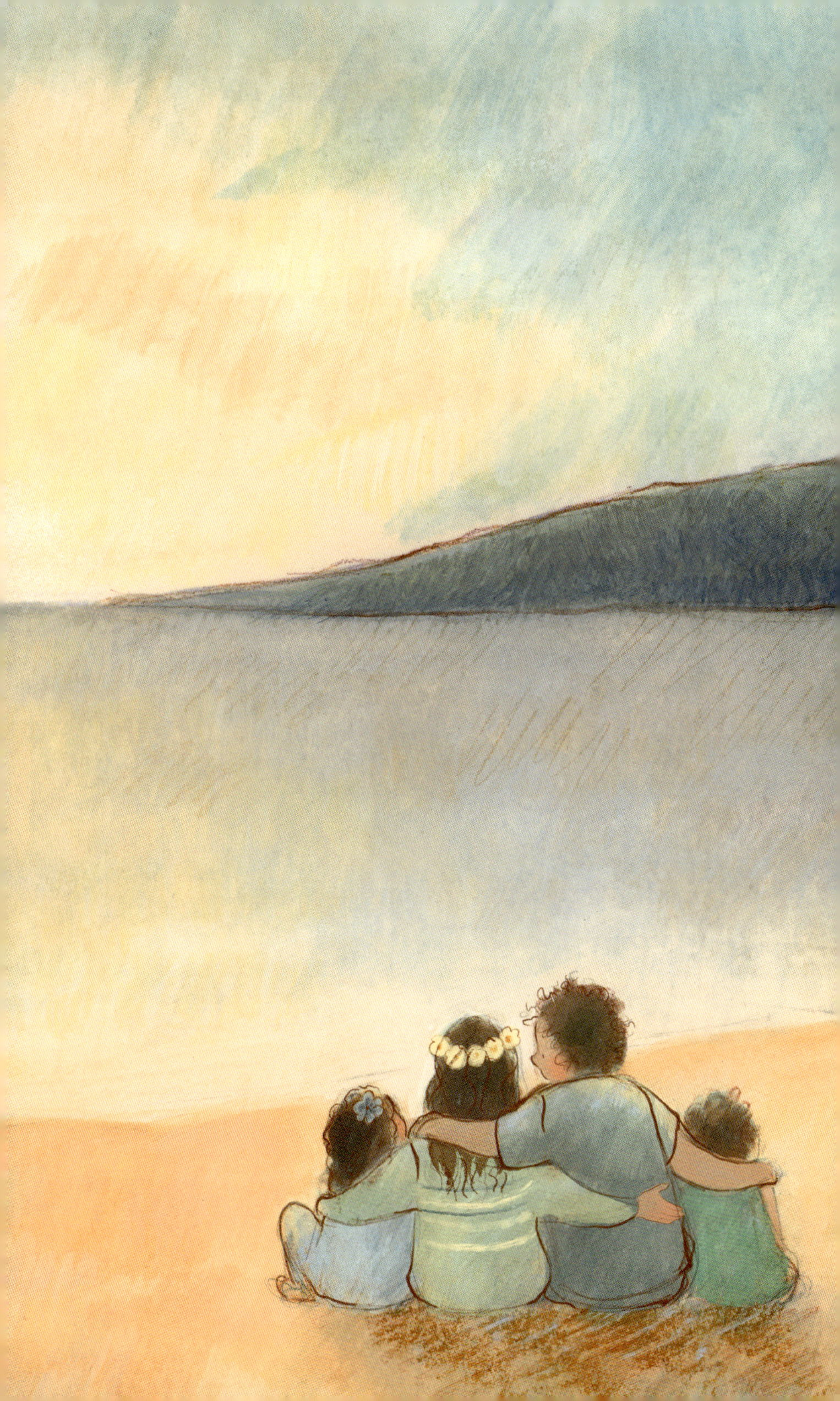

More Books from The Good and the Beautiful Library

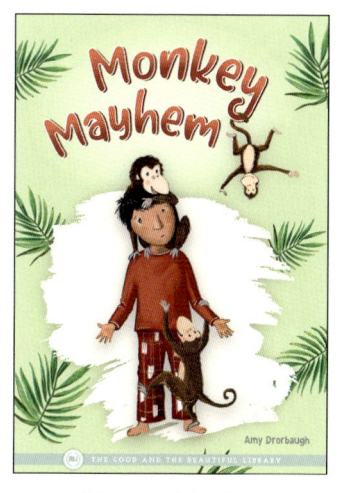

Monkey Mayhem
by Amy Drorbaugh

Brent's Bot
by Tessa Greene

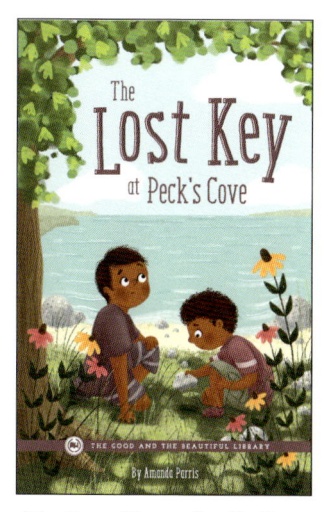

The Lost Key at Peck's Cove
by Amanda Parris

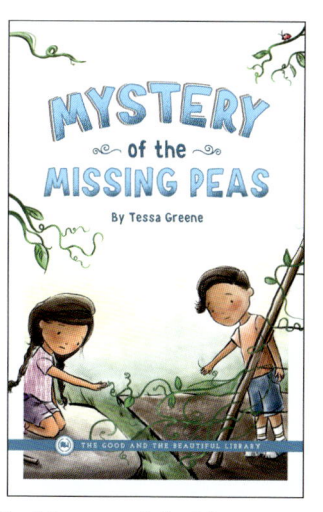

The Mystery of the Missing Peas
by Tessa Greene

goodandbeautiful.com